ORGANISTS CHARITABLE TRUST

Little Organ Book

NOVELLO

ACKNOWLEDGEMENTS

Michael White, for the initial idea.

Anne Marsden Thomas, for her advice on the content, and registration guidelines.

Novello & Company Limited and the Organists Charitable Trust gratefully acknowledge support from the
Ralph Vaughan Williams Trust, in commissioning new works by Iain Farrington and Thomas Hewitt Jones for the
Little Organ Book.

David Bednall was commissioned by the Organists Charitable Trust.

'White Note Paraphrase'
Music by James MacMillan
© Copyright 1998 Boosey & Hawkes Music Publishing Limited.
All Rights Reserved. International Copyright Secured.

'Cradle Song for Organ' is published by kind permission of the Literary Executors of the
Herbert Howells Trust.

Cover Image, photograph of the chancel organ at St. Giles' Cripplegate, London EC2
by Robert Andrews. Reproduced by permission.

Published by
Novello Publishing Limited
14-15 Berners Street, London W1T 3LJ, UK.

Exclusive Distributors:
Music Sales Limited
Distribution Centre, Newmarket Road, Bury St Edmunds, Suffolk IP33 3YB, UK.
Music Sales Corporation
257 Park Avenue South, New York, NY 10010, USA.
Music Sales Pty Limited
20 Resolution Drive, Caringbah, NSW 2229, Australia.

Order No. NOV016346
ISBN: 978-1-84938-681-4
This book © Copyright 2010 Novello Publishing Limited.

Music typesetting: John & Caroline Mortimer (Topscore Music Ltd.)
Design: Liz Barrand
Editor for Novello & Company: Rosie Moore

Printed in the EU.

CONTENTS

THE COMMISSIONED COMPOSERS

DAVID BEDNALL combines an extensive freelance career with the position of Sub-Organist at Bristol Cathedral, PhD studies in composition with John Pickard at Bristol University and the Directorship of The Bristol University Singers. The three CDs of his choral works on Regent Records have received widespread critical acclaim, and his compositions, notable for their vibrancy and immediacy, are increasingly in demand.

IAIN FARRINGTON enjoys an exceptionally busy and diverse career as pianist, organist, composer and arranger. He studied at the Royal Academy of Music, London and at Cambridge. As a composer, Iain has written chamber, instrumental, vocal and choral works. Notable successes include his organ works *Fiesta!* and *Animal Parade*, which have been performed in the USA, Canada, Australia, New Zealand, across Europe and the UK and have been recorded.

THOMAS HEWITT JONES is an award-winning composer of concert and commercial music. Winner of the BBC Young Composer competition in 2003, he has since had a number of pieces published. His ballet and instrumental music, in particular, is highly acclaimed. He has worked in Hollywood, and is composing the music for the 2012 Olympics Mascots films.

INTRODUCTION

The Organists Charitable Trust was founded in 1909, as *The Organists' Benevolent League* by Sir Frederick Bridge, Organist of Westminster Abbey, London (1882-1918). Its purpose was "to relieve by pecuniary assistance or otherwise organists and their dependents who are in distress through poverty". The Royal College of Organists supported the aims of the League, lending offices and clerical assistance, and by 1918 over £1,000 had been invested, putting the organisation on a sound basis. Over the years, the League has benefited from the generosity of many cathedrals, churches and individuals. Often, organists have donated the proceeds from one or more of their recitals. As a result of this generosity, the Organists Charitable Trust, as it became in 2009, has awarded grants to hundreds of organists. Beneficiaries' needs have changed with the times, but the Trust is still providing help, albeit in different ways.

In 2009 – the centenary year of its founding - the Trustees extended the aims of the charity to include, when the primary objectives have been met, support for organ tuition in cases of hardship.

With this in mind, the Trustees decided to mark the Centenary with a concert at the church of St. Giles without Cripplegate, Barbican, on 19 September 2009, and by the publication of this *Little Organ Book*. Amongst many musical delights at the Centenary concert, John Eady FRCO, an OCT beneficiary, gave the first performance of *Paean*, which had been wriiten for the occasion by one of the Trustees, Philip Moore.

Paean is the first work in a collection which consists of eleven relatively simple pieces of contrasting moods, seven drawn from the period covering the first hundred years of the Trust's existence and four representing the start of its second century. Also featured are new commissions by three of the younger generation of composers - *Fanfare-Processional* by David Bednall, *Bluesday* by Iain Farrington and *Carnival* by Thomas Hewitt Jones.

Published for the first time are Herbert Howells' *Cradle Song* and John Rutter's *Prelude: 'Te lucis ante terminum'*. The second half of the twentieth century is further reflected by contributions from James MacMillan, Peter Hurford and Paul Spicer.

Finally, acknowledging our inheritance, there are two works from the late nineteenth century by Bridge and Sir John Stainer (Organist of St. Paul's Cathedral, London (1872-1888)), both of whom made such an impact on the quality and performance of church music.

The Trustees hope and believe that this selection will appeal to a similarly wide cross-section of organists; they are most grateful to Novello for undertaking the publishing, to the RVW Trust, and to all the composers for generously agreeing that a proportion of the proceeds from sales will be donated to the Organists Charitable Trust.

Martin Neary
President, Organists Charitable Trust
July 2010

PAEAN

Suggested registration:
Sw. 8' 4' 2' Mixture
Gt. 8' 4' 2' Mixture Sw. to Gt. Ch. to Gt.
Ch. 8' 4' 2' Mixture
Ped. 16' 8' 4' Sw. to Ped. Gt. to Ped. Ch. to Ped.

PHILIP MOORE
(b. 1943)

Un poco allegro ♪ = *c.* 200-208

un poco rall.

a tempo

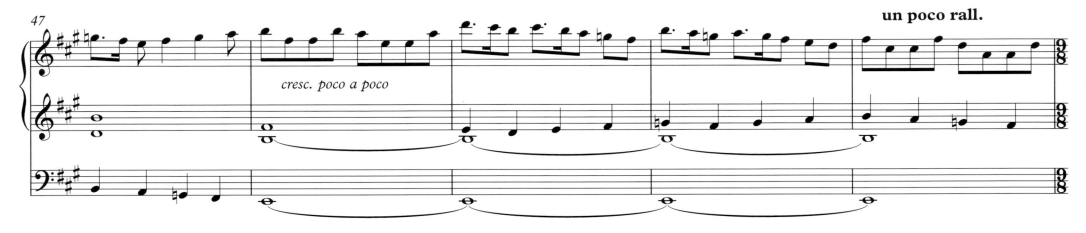

un poco rall.

Greenwich, CT, 19th June 2009

for Robert Houssart

BLUESDAY

IAIN FARRINGTON
(b. 1977)

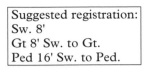

Suggested registration:
Sw. 8'
Gt 8' Sw. to Gt.
Ped 16' Sw. to Ped.

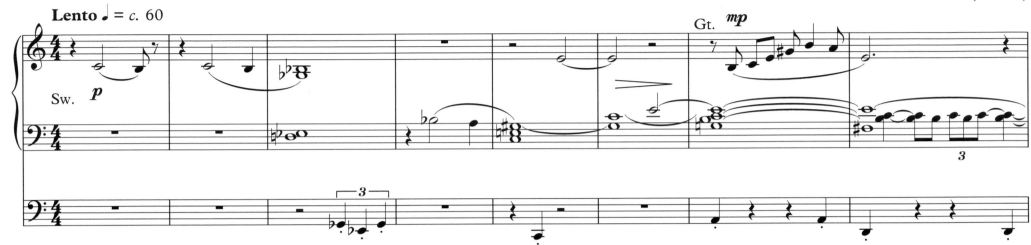

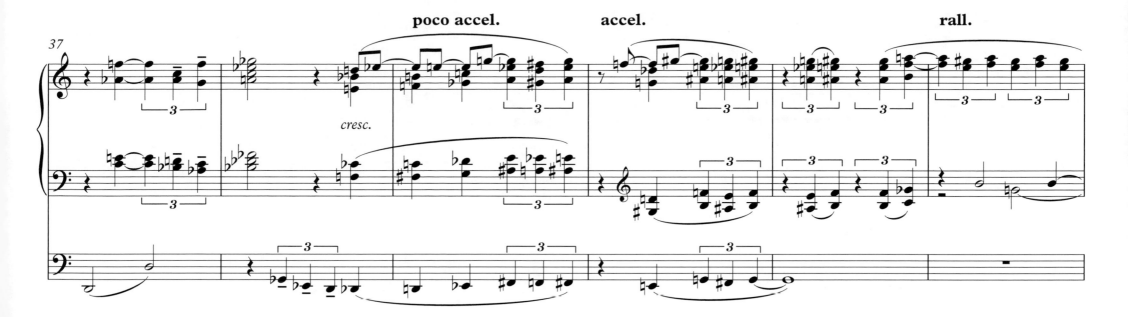

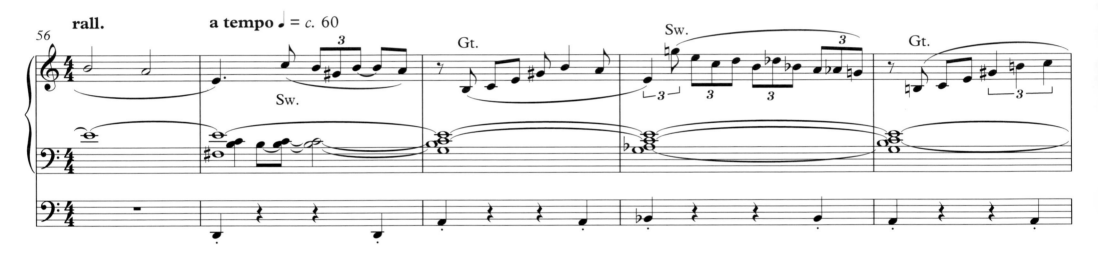

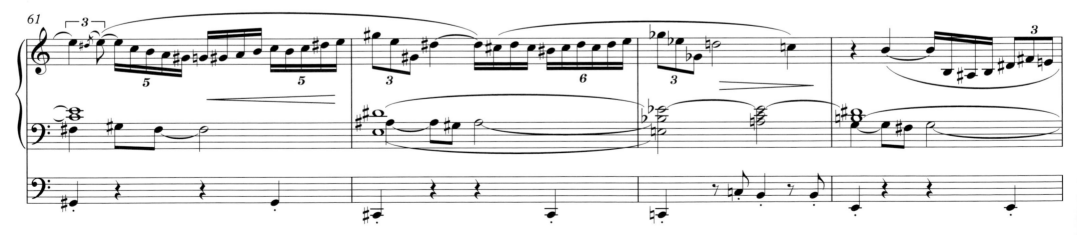

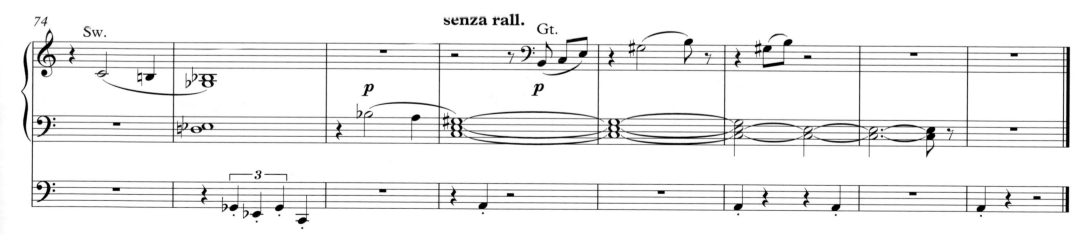

London, February 2010

written for Martin Neary, President of the Organists Charitable Trust

CARNIVAL

Suggested registration:
Sw. up to 8' reed (box shut)
Gt. 8' 4' foundations Sw. to Gt.
Ch. Solo Reed 8' Sw. to Ch.
Ped. 16' 8' 4' Sw. to Ped. Gt. to Ped.

THOMAS HEWITT JONES
(b. 1984)

With motion, with anticipation ♩ = *c.* 92–100

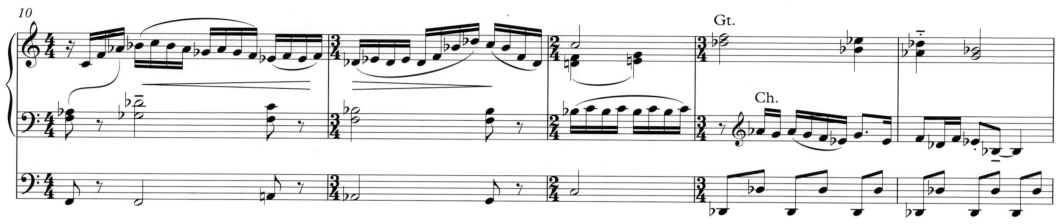

+ Sw. 4' Reed
+ Ped. 16' Reed

close box
+ Gt. Mixture   molto rit.   Tempo primo ♩ = c. 88-92
                                               reduce Gt. & Ped.

+ all Ped. reeds

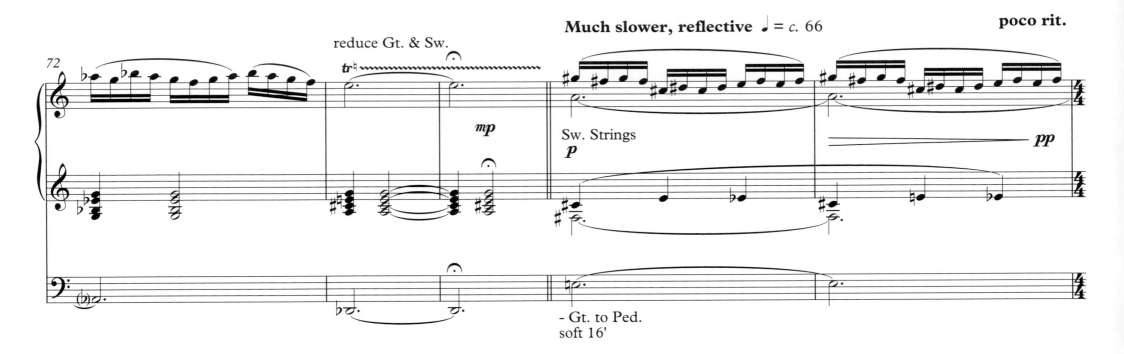

Dulwich, 2010

for John and Diane

WHITE NOTE PARAPHRASE

Suggested registration:
Sw. 8' 4' Reeds
Gt. 8' Flute
Ped. soft 16' Sw. to Ped.

JAMES MACMILLAN
(b. 1960)

★ all grace notes to be played on the beat

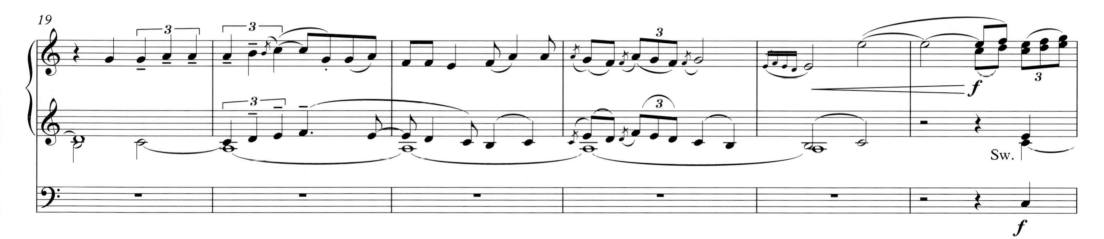

Glasgow, May 1994

FANFARE - PROCESSIONAL

Suggested registration:
Sw. up to 8' 4' Reeds and Mixtures
Gt. 8' 4' Foundations, 2' and Mixtures Sw. to Gt.
Ch. Solo Reed 8'
Ped. 16' 8' 4' Sw. to Ped. Gt. to Ped.

DAVID BEDNALL
(b. 1979)

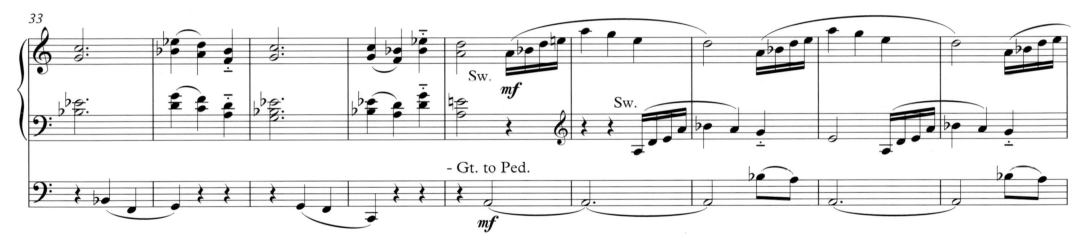

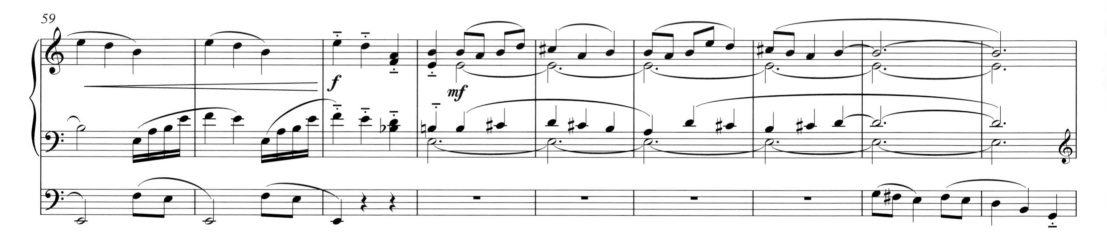

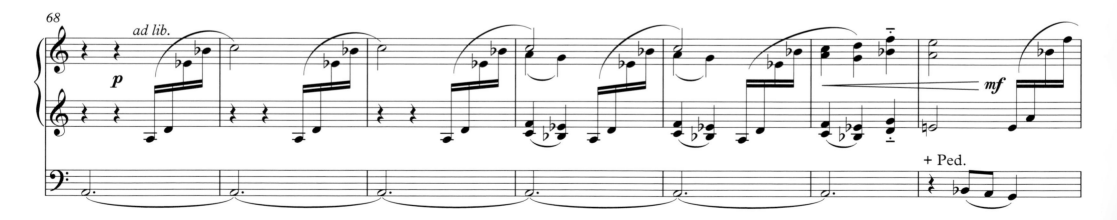

poco rit. _ _ _ _ _ Molto maestoso ♩ = c. 84

(Solo Reeds)

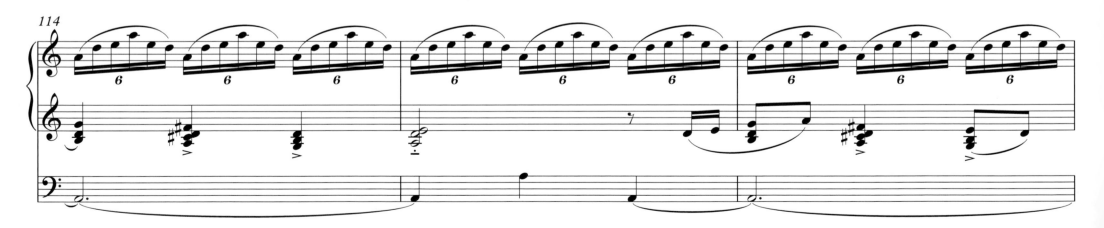

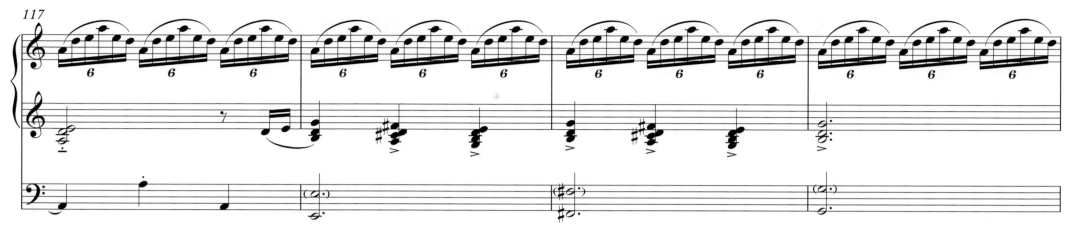

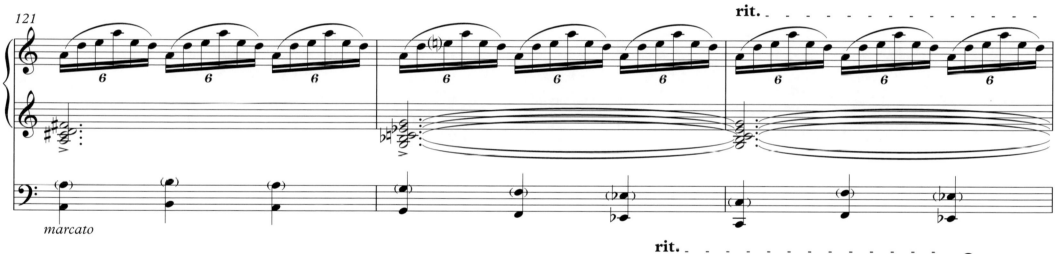

Clifton Village, 11th April 2010

in memoriam Hilary Gornall

PRELUDE: 'TE LUCIS ANTE TERMINUM'

Suggested registration:
Sw. 8' Flutes
Gt. Flute, Stopped Diapason Sw. to Gt.
Ped. 16' 8' Sw. to Ped. Gt. to Ped.

JOHN RUTTER
(b. 1945)

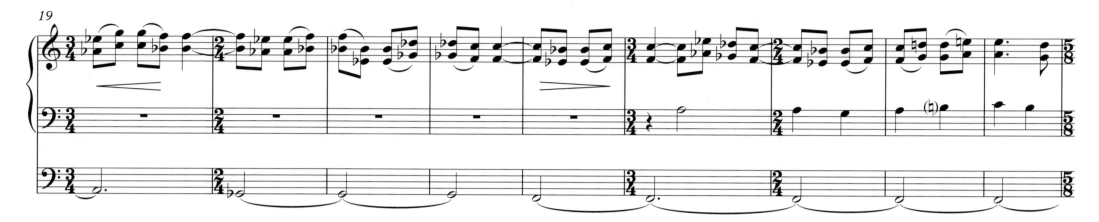

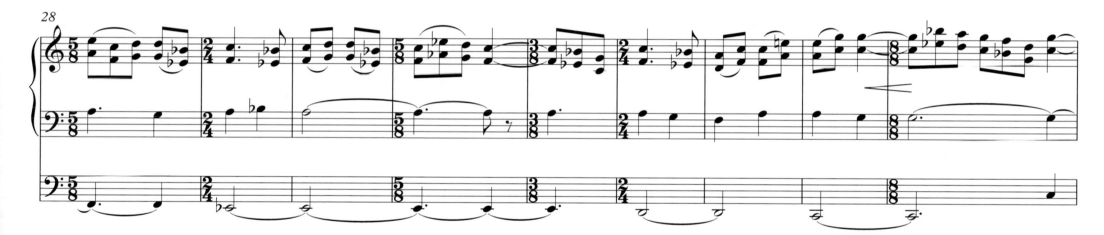

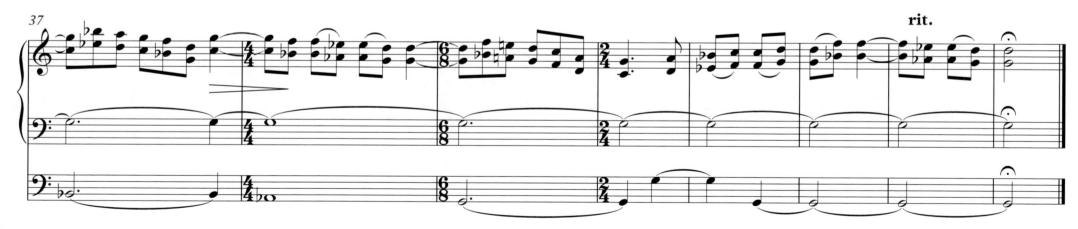

Cambridge, 1979

CRADLE SONG

Suggested registration:
Sw. 8' Strings
Gt. 8' Flute, Stopped Diapason Sw. to Gt.
Ch. 8' Sw. to Ch.
Ped. 16' 8' Sw. to Ped.

HERBERT HOWELLS
(1892-1983)

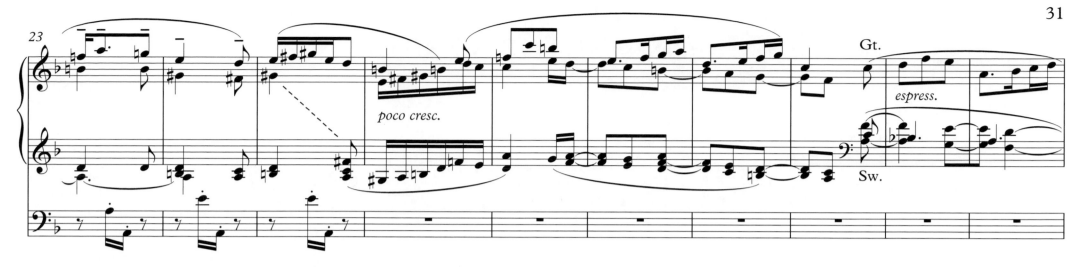

Lydney, Gloucestershire, 4th December 1913

for Virginia Graham

FANFARE FOR A BRIDE

PAUL SPICER
(b. 1952)

Suggested registration:
Sw. 8' 4' 2' Mixture
Gt. 8' 4' 2' Mixture Sw. to Gt.
Ped. 16' 8' 4' Sw. to Ped. Gt. to Ped.

★ The repeat is optional

Uppingham, 1970

DIALOGUE No. 2

Suggested registration:
Sw. 8' 4' 2' Flutes, Mixtures
Gt. 8' 4' 2' Principals, Mixtures Sw. to Gt. Ch. to Gt.
Ch. 8' 4' 2' Flutes
Ped. 16' 8' 4' Sw. to Ped. Gt. to Ped.

PETER HURFORD
(b. 1930)

- Gt. to Ped.

St. Albans, 1962

MEDITATION

for the organ or harmonium*

J. FREDERICK BRIDGE
(1844-1924)

Suggested registration:
Sw. 8' Flutes
Gt. 8' Flute, Stopped Diapason Sw. to Gt.
Ped. no pedal stops, but Sw. to Ped. Gt. to Ped. if required

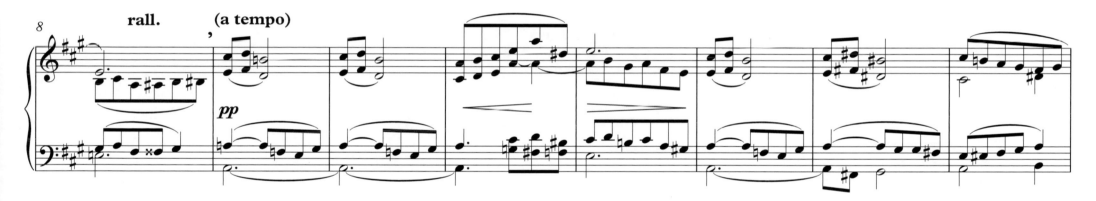

* Editor's note: Although Bridge wrote the Meditation for organ or harmonium, and presumably therefore for manuals only, it may help, because of the stretches required, to employ the pedals coupled to the manual stops but without any extra pedal stops.

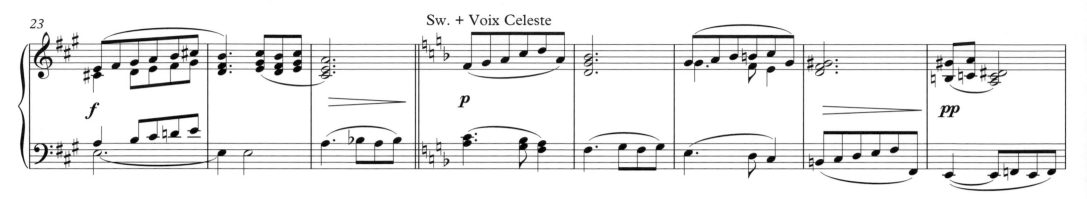

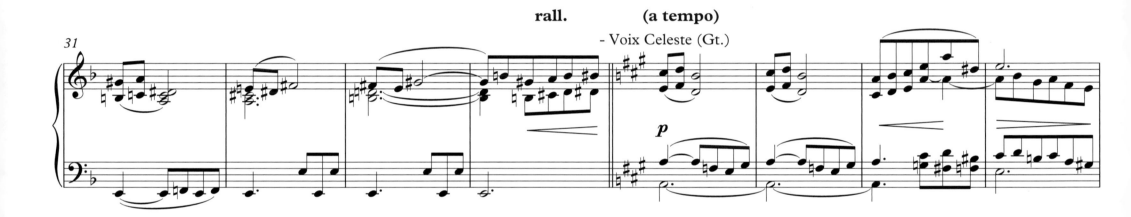

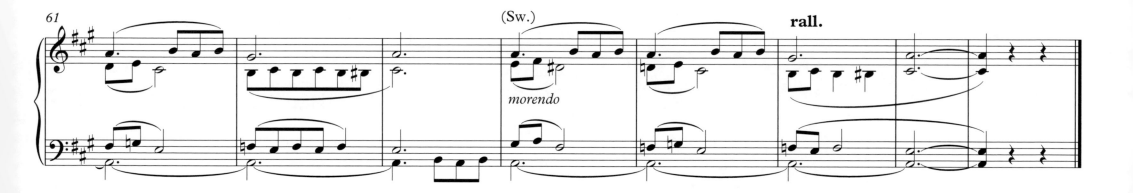

ANDANTE PATHETIQUE

Suggested registration:
Sw. 8' 4' Flutes
Gt. 8' Diapason Sw. to Gt.
Ped. 16'
Sw. to Ped. Gt. to Ped.

JOHN STAINER
(1840-1901)

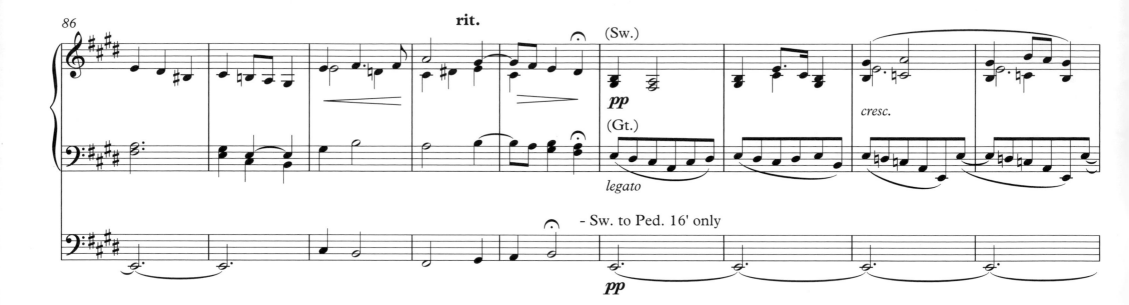

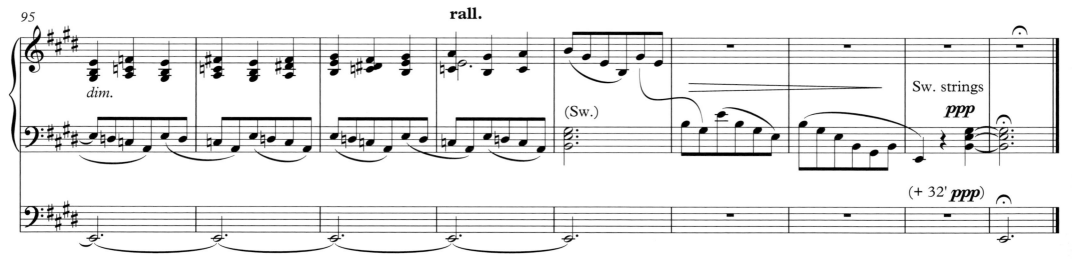

Florence, 1898